Ballerina
COOKBOOK

Ballerina
COOKBOOK

Janna DeVore

Photographs by Zac Williams

GIBBS SMITH
TO ENRICH AND INSPIRE HUMANKIND

For Elizabeth,
my ballerina princess

First Edition
15 14 13 12 11   5 4 3 2 1

Text © 2011 Janna DeVore
Photographs © 2011 Zac Williams

Published by
Gibbs Smith
P.O. Box 667
Layton, Utah 84041

1.800.835.4993 orders
www.gibbs-smith.com

Designed by Dawn DeVries Sokol
Manufactured in Shenzhen, China, in December 2010 by Toppan Printing Co. (SZ) Ltd.
Gibbs Smith books are printed on either recycled, 100% post-consumer waste, FSC-certified papers or on paper
produced from a sustainable PEFC-certified forest/controlled wood source. Learn more at www.pefc.org.

Library of Congress Cataloging-in-Publication Data

DeVore, Janna.
  Ballerina cookbook / Janna DeVore ; photographs by Zac Williams. — 1st ed.
     p. cm.
  ISBN 978-1-4236-0793-9
  1. Confectionary—Juvenile literature. 2. Childrens' parties—Juvenile literature. 3. Ballerinas—Juvenile
literature. I. Title.
  TX792.D48 2011
  641.8'6—dc22
                          2010030688

Contents

Introduction

You can enjoy an afternoon tea party, a dreamy bedtime snack, or a sweet dessert for your family and friends with more than 30 magical recipes—each inspired by a classic ballet. Before getting started making your ballerina treats, you'll want to remember:

• Always ask a parent or grown-up for permission to try out a recipe.

• Make sure you have an adult helper who can answer questions and help with tasks like melting chocolate, slicing and chopping, or using the oven.

• Read the entire recipe before you start. This way, you'll know exactly what to do and what ingredients you'll need to make the perfect treat.

• Get out everything you need to make the recipe before you start.

• Have fun!

Tiny Tutus

Serves 6

Tutus

- 4 egg whites, room temperature
- Pinch salt
- 1 cup sugar
- 2 teaspoons cornstarch
- 1 teaspoon white vinegar
- 1/2 teaspoon vanilla

Berries and Cream Topping

- 3 cups mixed berries
- 2 1/2 tablespoons sugar, divided
- 1 cup heavy cream

Preheat oven to 200 degrees F. Place a sheet of parchment paper on a large baking sheet. Use a 4-inch round bowl or ramekin to trace 6 circles on the parchment paper with a pencil. Turn parchment paper over so the circles are on the reverse side.

Place egg whites and salt in the bowl of an electric stand mixer fitted with the whisk attachment. Beat the egg whites on high speed until firm to the touch, 1 to 2 minutes. With the mixer on high, gradually add the sugar and continue beating until the mixture is very firm and forms stiff, shiny peaks, about 2 to 3 minutes.

Remove bowl from mixer, sprinkle cornstarch over the top, add vinegar and vanilla, and fold into stiff egg whites with a rubber spatula. Pile spoonfuls of the meringue onto the six circles. Smooth out the top of each circle with a spoon to make a flat disk—or tutu!

Bake tutus for 1 1/2 hours. Turn off oven and let the tutus cool in the oven for an additional hour. Tutus will be crisp on the outside and soft on the inside. You can store them in an air-tight container for several days or top with cream and berries and serve immediately.

To prepare berries, place washed fruit in a bowl and sprinkle with 1 1/2 tablespoons of the sugar. Let sit for 15 to 20 minutes.

continued

To prepare cream, pour into a bowl and beat on high speed with an electric mixer. Add 1 tablespoon sugar and continue beating until soft peaks form.

To serve tutus, place each meringue on a plate. Top equally with cream and berries. Drizzle extra berry juice over the top if desired.

Chocolate-Dipped Barres

Makes 18 to 24

- 24 pretzel rods
- 8 ounces semisweet chocolate
- 4 ounces white chocolate
- 3 tablespoons heavy cream
- Chopped nuts
- Colored sprinkles
- Mini M&Ms
- Shredded coconut
- Toffee pieces

Line a cookie sheet with parchment paper and set aside.

Bring a pan of water to a simmer over medium heat. Break chocolate and white chocolate into pieces and place in a medium glass bowl. Add cream and place bowl over the simmering water. Make sure the water doesn't boil or touch the bowl. Stir chocolate and cream occasionally, until chocolate is melted and mixture is smooth.

Remove bowl from simmering water. Tilt bowl slightly and dip one half of the first pretzel in the chocolate. Swirl several times to coat well. Place dipped pretzel on parchment paper, then sprinkle with one or any combination of toppings.

Repeat with remaining pretzels and chocolate.

Pointe Shoe Cookies

Makes 2 to 3 dozen cookies

- 1 cup butter, softened
- 1 cup sugar
- 2 tablespoons cream cheese, softened
- 1 egg, well beaten
- 1 1/2 teaspoons vanilla extract
- 1/2 cup milk
- 1 tablespoon baking powder
- 1/2 teaspoon salt
- 3 cups flour
- 1 recipe Cream Cheese Frosting
- Candies for decorating

Cream Cheese Frosting

- 6 ounces cream cheese, softened
- 2 cups powdered sugar
- 1 1/2 teaspoons vanilla extract

To make cookies, in a large bowl, cream butter, sugar, and cream cheese until light and fluffy, about 2 minutes. Mix in egg, vanilla, and milk until combined. Add dry ingredients and mix on low speed until combined. Wrap dough in plastic wrap and chill in the refrigerator for at least an hour or up to one day.

Preheat oven to 375 degrees F.

Divide dough into smaller sections. Roll out one section to an 1/8 inch thickness on a floured surface. Cut out shapes with a slipper-shaped cookie cutter. Gather dough scraps and roll out again. Place cutout cookies on an ungreased baking sheet and bake 7 to 10 minutes. Let cookies rest on hot baking sheets after removing from oven for 10 minutes. Cookies shouldn't brown.

Remove to wire racks to cool completely, then frost with Cream Cheese Frosting.

To make frosting, beat cream cheese, powdered sugar, and vanilla with an electric mixer until light and fluffy, 3 to 4 minutes. If desired, tint frosting with a few drops of red food coloring. Decorate the cookies with tiny candies.

Ballerina Buns

Makes 3 dozen

Dough

1 cup water

1 cup cold butter, cut into chunks

3/4 cup sugar

2 teaspoons salt

1 cup cold water

2 (0.25-ounce) packets yeast

1/2 cup warm water

4 eggs, beaten

8 cups flour

Filling

1 cup dark brown sugar

3 tablespoons ground cinnamon

1/2 cup butter, softened

Prepare dough the night before you want to serve the buns. In a large pot over medium-high heat, bring 1 cup water to a boil. Add butter, sugar, and salt and remove from heat. Add 1 cup cold water and let mixture cool to lukewarm, about 5 minutes.

While mixture cools, dissolve yeast in the 1/2 cup warm water in a separate bowl. Let mixture rest 5 minutes, until foamy.

When butter and sugar mixture is lukewarm, add eggs and yeast. Stir well to make sure sugar is dissolved. Gradually mix in flour with a wooden spoon until well mixed. The dough will be very soft and sticky. Cover pot with a lid or plastic wrap and refrigerate at least 4 hours or overnight. This allows enough time for dough to rise almost to the top of the pan.

When ready to shape rolls, coat 3 rimmed baking sheets with nonstick cooking spray and set aside. Combine brown sugar and cinnamon in a small bowl and set aside.

Remove dough from refrigerator and use a rubber spatula to scrape it out of the pot onto a well-floured surface. Divide dough into 3 pieces. Dust the countertop or a bread board with additional flour and roll out first piece in a 15 x 6-inch rectangle.

Glaze

1/2 cup butter, melted

3 cups powdered sugar

1 teaspoon vanilla

4 to 5 tablespoons cream

Spread one third of the softened butter over the rectangle and sprinkle with one third of the cinnamon-sugar mixture. Use your fingers to slightly press mixture into dough. Roll up the dough tightly, pinching edges together when finished. Slice roll into 12 rounds.

Place rounds on prepared baking sheet and cover with a clean towel. Repeat with remaining pieces of dough. Let rolls raise 2 to 3 hours.

Preheat oven to 375 degrees F. Bake each sheet 15 to 20 minutes, until rolls are golden brown and cinnamon mixture is bubbly. Remove from oven and cool 10 to 15 minutes before glazing.

Prepare glaze by whisking together melted butter, powdered sugar, and vanilla in a small bowl. Gradually whisk in cream, 1 tablespoon at a time, until glaze reaches a smooth, creamy consistency. Pour over warm rolls and serve immediately.

Pas de Deux
Ice Cream Sandwich Cookies

Makes 12 small ice cream sandwich cookies

- 1.5 quarts premium vanilla ice cream, softened slightly
- ¾ cup bottled lemon curd
- 1 package purchased shortbread cookies
- 1 cup sugar
- 4 teaspoons lemon zest

Several hours before serving, spoon softened ice cream into a large mixing bowl and stir in lemon curd until well combined. Return ice cream to carton or place in a freezer-safe container and return to freezer.

Combine sugar and lemon zest in the bowl of a food processor and process until zest and sugar are well mixed and slightly damp. Pour lemon-sugar into a shallow bowl.

Line a large platter with parchment paper and place platter in freezer.

Remove ice cream from freezer and soften slightly before assembling cookie sandwiches. Scoop a spoonful of ice cream on top of one cookie. Place a second cookie on top of ice cream and press down so that ice cream reaches the edge of both cookies.

Roll edges of ice cream in lemon-sugar and place cookie on platter in the freezer so it doesn't start to melt. Repeat until you've used all the ice cream or have made the number of cookies desired. Serve immediately or store in freezer until ready to serve.

Pumpkin Pirouette Mousse

Serves 8

- 8 ounces cream cheese, softened
- $1/4$ cup sugar
- 1 (16-ounce) can pure pumpkin (not pumpkin pie filling)
- 1 small box vanilla instant pudding
- 2 teaspoons pumpkin pie spice
- 1 cup milk
- 1 cup heavy cream
- 1 tablespoon sugar
- 10 to 12 gingersnap cookies, crushed (optional)

In a medium bowl, mix cream cheese and sugar with an electric mixer until smooth and creamy. Beat in pumpkin. Add pudding mix and pumpkin pie spice and mix well. Gradually beat in milk until incorporated well. Set aside.

Pour cream and sugar into a medium bowl and beat on high speed until soft peaks form.

Using a rubber spatula, fold half of the whipped cream into the pumpkin mixture.

Spoon $1/2$ cup of the pumpkin mousse into 8 individual serving dishes. Chill until ready to serve. To serve, top with a dollop of remaining whipped cream. If desired, sprinkle with crushed cookies.

Christmas Eve Treats

Makes about 24 cupcakes

- 3 cups flour
- 1/2 teaspoon salt
- 1 1/2 teaspoons baking powder
- 1 cup butter, softened
- 2 cups sugar
- 4 eggs, room temperature
- 1 cup milk
- 1 teaspoon vanilla extract
- 1 recipe Smooth Vanilla Buttercream
- 1/2 cup to 3/4 cup pomegranate seeds

Smooth Vanilla Buttercream

- 1 1/2 cups butter, softened
- 3 tablespoons heavy cream
- 2 1/2 teaspoons vanilla extract
- 1/4 teaspoon salt
- 6 cups powdered sugar

Preheat oven to 350 degrees F. Line two muffin tins with paper liners and set aside.

In a small bowl, whisk together flour, salt, and baking powder; set aside. In a large bowl, cream butter with an electric mixer on medium speed until butter is smooth. Add sugar, 1/2 cup at a time, and beat until the mixture is light and fluffy, about 3 minutes. Add the eggs, one at a time, beating after each addition. Add half of the flour and mix until incorporated. Add half of the milk and the vanilla and mix well. Repeat with remaining flour and milk. Do not overmix. Spoon batter into cupcake liners, filling them 3/4 full. Bake 20 to 25 minutes, or until a toothpick inserted in center of a cupcake comes out clean.

Let cupcakes cool for 15 minutes, and then remove from muffin tins to cool completely on a wire rack.

Frost with Smooth Vanilla Buttercream. Pat pomegranate seeds dry with a paper towel then sprinkle over cupcakes.

To make the frosting, place butter, cream, vanilla, and salt in a large bowl. Using an electric mixer on medium-high speed, beat until smooth, about 2 minutes.

Reduce to low and add powdered sugar. Beat 2 minutes, then increase speed to medium-high, and beat another 5 minutes, until frosting is very light and fluffy.

Spiced Nuts

Serves 12

- 1 egg white
- 1 teaspoon water
- 1 ½ tablespoons brown sugar
- 1 teaspoon ground cinnamon
- ¼ teaspoon salt
- ¼ teaspoon cayenne pepper (optional)
- ¼ teaspoon ground cumin (optional)
- ¼ teaspoon ground coriander (optional)
- 3 cups unsalted pecans, almonds, and cashews

Preheat oven to 325 degrees F. Line a baking sheet with parchment paper and coat paper lightly with nonstick cooking spray; set aside.

Whisk egg white and water in a small bowl until mixture looks foamy and bubbly. Stir in brown sugar, cinnamon, and salt. Add cayenne, cumin, and coriander, if using. Add nuts and toss with a spoon until nuts are well coated.

Pour nuts onto parchment paper and spread evenly across surface of pan.

Bake 20 to 25 minutes. Nuts should be golden and appear dry when finished. Remove from oven and cool. Can be stored in an airtight container up to 2 weeks.

The Mouse King's Delight

Makes 4 dessert sandwiches

- 8 slices sourdough bread, sliced 1/2-inch thick
- Butter, softened
- Strawberry fruit spread or preserves
- 8 ounces brie, sliced

To prepare each sandwich, spread each of 4 slices of bread with softened butter; set aside.

Spread each of remaining 4 slices of bread with strawberry spread or preserves. Top the preserves with sliced brie. Top brie with the buttered bread, making sure the buttered side faces out.

Place sandwiches, buttered side down, in a nonstick skillet or griddle. Spread softened butter over the top slice of each sandwich. Heat skillet to medium heat. Let sandwich brown until golden, pressing down gently on the bread with a spatula. When bottoms are golden brown, flip with a spatula to brown the other side.

Serve immediately.

Snow-Flaked
Ice Cream Balls

Makes 1 to 2 dozen

- 1.5 quarts peppermint or vanilla bean ice cream, softened
- 1 bag flaked, sweetened coconut
- 1 recipe Heavenly Hot Fudge Sauce

Heavenly Hot Fudge Sauce

- 1 (14-ounce) bag Kraft caramels, unwrapped
- 2 (12-ounce) cans evaporated milk
- 2 cups butter
- 2 cups sugar
- Dash salt
- 1/3 cup dark corn syrup
- 1 (12-ounce) package semisweet chocolate chips
- 1 teaspoon vanilla extract

To make the ice cream balls, the morning before serving, line a rimmed baking sheet with parchment paper and set aside. Scoop ice cream from carton and form into balls. You can use a large or small scoop and make balls any size you want. If you have really clean hands, you can even shape the balls by hand. Use as much ice cream as needed to make the number of snowballs you need. Place the balls on baking sheet and return to the freezer until solid.

When ready to serve, dump the coconut into a 9 x 13-inch pan. Remove ice cream balls from the freezer and roll in coconut. Press coconut onto the sides of the balls to help it stick. To serve, drizzle hot fudge over a plate, place ice cream balls on top of the sauce, then drizzle liberally with more sauce.

To make the hot fudge sauce, place all ingredients except vanilla in a large, microwave-proof bowl. Heat on high for 2 minutes. Stir, then heat another 2 minutes. Repeat until mixture is melted. Stir in vanilla and beat with an electric mixer on medium speed for 2 to 3 minutes. Extra sauce may be refrigerated for up to 6 weeks or frozen up to 6 months. Reheat before serving.

Sugar Plum Fairy Pops

Makes 36 pops

- 1 prepared cheesecake, purchased or homemade
- 36 sucker sticks (available at most craft stores)
- 12 ounces semisweet chocolate
- 1 tablespoon shortening
- Sprinkles (optional)
- Chopped nuts (optional)

Line a baking sheet with parchment paper. Use a tablespoon to scoop out a 1-inch ball of cheesecake. With clean hands, shape the portion into a ball. Roll with your hands until the ball is smooth and place on prepared baking sheet. Repeat to make about 36 balls.

Place a sucker stick in the top of each cheesecake ball. Make sure the stick goes almost through the other side, but not quite. Place the baking sheet in the freezer and freeze balls until hard, about 3 hours.

When ready to dip pops, break chocolate into pieces and put it in a microwave-safe bowl with the shortening. Microwave on high for 30 second. Remove and stir. Repeat until chocolate is melted, smooth, and creamy.

Remove pops from freezer. Dip each pop in chocolate, tilting bowl as needed to cover the cheesecake ball. Hold pop upright so chocolate drips down to cover the entire pop. Return pop to parchment-lined pan and sprinkle with toppings, if using. Repeat with remaining pops.

Store in refrigerator until ready to serve.

Russian Dancers' Peppermint Bark

Makes 2 dozen pieces

- 6 ounces Ghirardelli semisweet chocolate
- 2 teaspoons shortening
- 6 ounces Ghirardelli white chocolate
- 1/2 cup crushed peppermint candies or candy canes

To crush peppermints, place in a ziplock bag and smash with a meat mallet or rolling pin; set aside.

Line a 9 x 13-inch baking dish with aluminum foil, making sure the foil hangs out over the edges of the pan; set aside.

Have an adult help you bring a pot of water to a simmer over medium heat. Break dark chocolate into pieces and place in a medium glass bowl. Add 1 teaspoon shortening to chocolate and place bowl over the pot of simmering water. Make sure the water doesn't boil or touch the bowl. Stir chocolate occasionally, until mixture is smooth and melted.

Once it is melted, pour dark chocolate into prepared pan and spread it evenly over the surface with a rubber spatula. Place pan in the refrigerator for 30 minutes to harden.

Bring the pot of water to a simmer again. Repeat process for melting chocolate for the white chocolate.

Remove pan of dark chocolate from refrigerator. Pour white chocolate over the top and use a rubber spatula to spread it evenly over the dark chocolate. Sprinkle with crushed peppermint candies, press candies lightly into the chocolate, and return pan to refrigerator for another 30 to 45 minutes.

continued

After chocolate has hardened, remove pan from refrigerator and use the foil hanging over the edge of the pan to lift out candy. Peel the foil off the candy and break candy into pieces. Peppermint bark can be stored in an airtight container up to 2 weeks.

Waltz of the Flowers Party

Serves 8

Fruit Flower Bouquet

1 fresh pineapple

Flower-shaped
  cookie cutter

1 cantaloupe, halved
  and seeded

1 bunch purple grapes

3 to 4 cups whole
  strawberries,
  stems removed

Bamboo skewers

Play dough or floral foam

Vase or other container
  to hold your flowers

Prepare Fruit Flower Bouquet: Ask an adult to help you slice the pineapple into $\frac{1}{2}$-inch thick slices. Use the cookie cutter to cut out a flower shape from each slice. Set flowers aside on a baking sheet or cutting board while you prepare the rest of the fruit.

Using a melon baller, scoop out balls of the cantaloupe until you have used all the fruit. Slice enough balls in half to have a center for each of your pineapple flowers.

Thread a skewer through the middle of a pineapple flower; the skewer should poke through the top of the pineapple about a half inch. Put a melon ball half on top of the skewer, making sure the skewer doesn't poke through the top of the melon ball. Repeat with remaining pineapple flowers.

Take a skewer and thread 6 or 7 grapes on it. Repeat to make a total of 9 or 10 skewers.

Take a skewer and stick it into the top of 1 strawberry. Don't let the skewer poke through the top of the berry. Repeat to make 14 or 15 more strawberry skewers.

Now that your fruit is ready, ask an adult to help you shape a ball of play dough or a piece of floral foam to fit in the bottom of your vase or other container.

Easy Creamy Fruit Dip

1 (8-ounce) package
  cream cheese, softened

1 (7-ounce) jar
  marshmallow crème

3 (6-ounce) cartons Yoplait
  red raspberry yogurt

Insert the skewers, one at a time, into the play dough or floral foam to make your flower bouquet arrangement.

Toss remaining fruit in bowl to serve alongside the bouquet.

Prepare Easy Creamy Fruit Dip: In a medium bowl, beat cream cheese with an electric mixer until smooth. Gradually mix in marshmallow crème until well blended. Stir in yogurt and mix well. Transfer to a small serving bowl and serve with Fruit Bouquet. Store leftover dip in the refrigerator.

Mother Ginger's Shining Stars

Makes 8 to 10 stars

Gingerbread

- 1 1/2 cups flour
- 2 teaspoons ground ginger
- 1 teaspoon cocoa powder
- 1 teaspoon ground cinnamon
- 1/2 teaspoon ground cloves
- 1/2 teaspoon ground nutmeg
- 1/2 teaspoon ground allspice
- 1/2 teaspoon baking soda
- 1/2 teaspoon salt
- 3/4 cup molasses
- 3/4 cup sugar
- 1/2 cup butter, melted
- 1 egg
- 1 cup buttermilk
- Star-shaped cookie cutter

Topping

- 1 cup heavy cream
- 1 tablespoon sugar
- 4 or 5 bananas, sliced
- Ground cinnamon or nutmeg

Preheat oven to 350 degrees F. Line a 9 x 13-inch baking pan with aluminum foil so the edges hang over the handles of the pan. Coat the foil with nonstick cooking spray.

In a medium bowl, whisk together dry ingredients; set aside.

In a large bowl, beat molasses, sugar, and melted butter on low speed until combined well, about 2 minutes.

Beat in the egg and buttermilk until combined, about 1 minute. Add the flour mixture and beat on low speed until batter is smooth and thick, about 2 minutes.

Pour batter into prepared pan and smooth the top. Bake 25 to 30 minutes, until a toothpick inserted in center comes out almost clean.

Let cake cool in pan at least 1 hour. Remove cake from pan by lifting foil handles and moving it to a countertop.

Spray a star-shaped cookie cutter with nonstick cooking spray, then use it to cut out pieces of the cake.

Prepare topping by whipping cream and sugar in a medium bowl on high speed until soft peaks form. To serve, plate each star and top with a dollop of whipped cream, 1/4 cup sliced bananas, and a sprinkle of cinnamon or nutmeg.

Spanish Dancers'
White Hot Chocolate

Serves 4

- 3 cups half-and-half
- 1 cup milk
- 1 cup plus 1 tablespoon white chocolate chips
- 1 teaspoon vanilla extract
- ¼ teaspoon ground nutmeg, plus additional for garnishing
- Freshly whipped cream or Reddi Whip, for topping

Combine half-and-half, milk, white chocolate chips, vanilla, and nutmeg in a medium saucepan and heat slowly over medium heat, whisking often.

When mixture is warm, whisk vigorously until it is frothy and chocolate is melted. Pour into mugs. Top with a dollop of whipped cream or a shot of Reddi Whip. Sprinkle nutmeg over top and serve.

Dainty Fairy Gift Cakes

Serves 8

- 1 box devil's food cake mix
- 1 small box chocolate instant pudding
- 1 cup sour cream
- 4 eggs
- ½ cup vegetable oil
- 1½ cups water
- 1½ cups semisweet chocolate chips
- 1 cup heavy cream
- 1 tablespoon sugar
- 2 cups fresh or frozen raspberries

Preheat oven to 350 degrees F. Coat 8 ramekins with cooking spray and place on a large, rimmed baking sheet; set aside.

In a large bowl, combine cake mix, instant pudding, sour cream, eggs, oil, water, and chocolate chips. Mix with a wooden spoon until combined well; do not overmix. Divide batter evenly between ramekins.

Bake 30 to 35 minutes, until toothpick inserted in center comes out almost clean.

Let cakes cool in ramekins for 10 to 15 minutes. To serve, run a butter knife around the edge of the ramekin, then invert onto a dessert plate and remove ramekin.

Beat cream and sugar together in a medium bowl on high speed until soft peaks form. Top each cake with a generous dollop of the whipped cream and ¼ cup raspberries.

Aurora's Pink Princess
Birthday Cake

Serves 8 to 10

- 1 large purchased
  angel food cake
- 1 small package
  strawberry gelatin
- 1 cup boiling water
- 1 pound frozen
  strawberry slices
- 1 cup (½ pint)
  heavy cream
- 2 tablespoons sugar
- Red food coloring
- Fresh strawberries,
  for garnish

Slice a 1-inch horizontal layer off the top of the cake and set aside. Hollow out the remaining cake, making a trough that goes around the entire cake. The trough should be centered between the outside and inside diameter of the cake. Tear hollowed-out cake into bite-sized pieces and set aside.

Place gelatin in a medium bowl and pour boiling water over top. Stir until completely dissolved. Add frozen berries and reserved cake pieces to gelatin and stir well. Mixture will begin to thicken right away. If it doesn't begin to thicken, let it chill in the refrigerator for 20 to 30 minutes. Fill trough with strawberry mixture and replace cake top.

In another bowl, whip cream and sugar together until firm peaks form. Add a drop or two of red food coloring. Frost cake with whipped cream. Slice fresh strawberries in half and decorate top of cake as desired.

Sleepytime Vanilla Steamers

Serves 4

- 4 cups whole milk
- 1 1/2 teaspoons vanilla
- 1/2 teaspoon sugar
- 1/2 teaspoon ground cinnamon
- 1/4 teaspoon ground nutmeg
- Pinch salt

Bring the milk to a simmer in a medium saucepan over medium heat. Just before milk looks like it will boil, remove from heat and add remaining ingredients. Whisk vigorously with a wire whisk until milk is frothy on top. Pour into mugs and serve immediately.

Prince Florimund's
Spell Snappers

Makes 2 to 3 dozen

- ³/₄ cup butter, softened
- 1 cup sugar, plus ¹/₄ cup for coating cookies
- 1 egg
- ¹/₄ cup molasses
- 2 cups flour
- 2 teaspoons baking soda
- 1 teaspoon ground cinnamon
- 1 teaspoon ground ginger
- 1 teaspoon ground cloves
- ¹/₂ teaspoon ground nutmeg
- ¹/₂ teaspoon ground allspice

Preheat oven to 325 degrees F.

In a large bowl, cream butter and 1 cup sugar together until light and fluffy. Add egg and molasses and mix well. Add flour, soda, and spices and mix to combine.

Pour the ¹/₄ cup sugar into a small bowl. Form dough into 1-inch balls. Roll each ball in sugar and place on prepared cookie sheets. Bake 10 to 12 minutes. Cool slightly on pans, then remove to wire racks to cool completely.

The Bluebird's Cobbler

Serves 8 to 10

Fruit Filling

- 6 cups fresh or frozen blueberries, thawed and drained
- 1 tablespoon freshly squeezed lemon juice
- ½ cup sugar
- ½ teaspoon ground cinnamon
- ¼ teaspoon ground nutmeg
- 4 teaspoons cornstarch

Biscuit Topping

- 1½ cups flour
- ¼ cup sugar, plus 2 teaspoons
- 1½ teaspoons baking powder
- ½ teaspoon baking soda
- ¼ teaspoon salt
- ⅛ teaspoon ground nutmeg
- 1½ teaspoons lemon zest
- 5 tablespoons butter, melted
- ¾ cup cold buttermilk
- 1 teaspoon lemon juice

Preheat oven to 400 degrees F.

To prepare fruit filling, measure blueberries into a large bowl. Sprinkle lemon juice over the top and set aside. In a small bowl, whisk together sugar, cinnamon, nutmeg, and cornstarch. Pour dry ingredients over berries and toss gently to coat. Transfer berries to a 2-quart casserole or similar baking dish. Set aside while preparing biscuit topping.

To prepare biscuit topping, in a medium bowl, whisk together flour, ¼ cup sugar, baking powder, baking soda, salt, nutmeg, and lemon zest. In a separate small bowl, stir together melted butter and cold buttermilk. Pour liquid mixture into dry ingredients and combine gently, using a rubber spatula.

Place spoonfuls of the biscuit dough evenly over top of berries. Brush the tops with lemon juice and sprinkle with remaining 2 teaspoons sugar.

Bake 25 to 30 minutes, until top is golden brown and fruit is bubbly. Cool slightly, then serve warm with whipped cream or vanilla ice cream.

Fairy-Tale Fantasy

Serves 8 to 10

- 15 cups popped corn (not microwave popcorn)
- 3 cups pink melting candy, such as Wilton Candy Melts

Sift through popped corn to remove any stray kernels. Place popcorn in a large mixing bowl and set aside. If desired, you can divide the popcorn into 2 bowls and melt 2 different colors of candy for each bowl.

Place melting candy in a small, microwave-proof bowl and microwave on 50 percent power for 30 seconds. Stir candy and microwave at 50 percent power another 30 seconds. Repeat until candy is smooth and melted. Pour over popcorn and stir with a wooden spoon or spatula until popcorn is coated with candy.

Spread popcorn out on baking sheets and let cool to room temperature for an hour or so. Pink and mint green make pretty color combinations; but you can choose any color you'd like.

A Royal Toast

Serves 30

- 1 large can frozen concentrate limeade
- 7 cans water
- 4 cups sugar
- Red food coloring
- 2 (2-liter) bottles lemon-lime soda

In a large bowl or stockpot, combine limeade, water, and sugar. Mix well to dissolve sugar. Add red food coloring until mixture reaches a color slightly darker than you would like it to look in the punch bowl. Carefully pour the mixture into a clean, dry 4-quart plastic container with a lid. Freeze at least overnight.

When ready to serve, let mixture thaw for about 30 to 45 minutes in container; transfer to a punch bowl. Dilute with soda, pouring slowly and stopping frequently to break up clumps of slush. Ladle into cups and serve.

Peanut Butter Party Favors

Makes 2 dozen

- 4 ounces Ghirardelli white chocolate
- ½ cup creamy peanut butter
- 16 ounces Ghirardelli semisweet chocolate
- 2 teaspoons shortening
- 2 tablespoons unsalted roasted peanuts, chopped

Line 2 mini muffin tins with paper liners and set aside. Bring a pot of water to a simmer over medium heat. Break white chocolate into pieces and place in a medium glass bowl. Add peanut butter and place bowl over the pot of simmering water. Make sure the water doesn't boil or touch the bowl. Stir until mixture is smooth and melted. Set aside to cool slightly.

Return the pot of water to a simmer and break dark chocolate into pieces in another glass bowl. Add shortening and place bowl over the simmering water. Remember not to let the water boil or touch the bowl. Stir chocolate occasionally, until smooth and melted.

Remove chocolate from heat. Spoon 1 to 2 teaspoons chocolate into bottom of each paper liner. Spoon an equal amount of the peanut butter mixture on top of chocolate. Layer remaining chocolate over peanut butter. Sprinkle tops with chopped nuts. Put muffin tins in the freezer for 15 to 20 minutes to harden. Remove from freezer, let cups come to room temperature, and serve.

The Prince's Birthday Toast

Serves 12

- 1 orange
- 1 lemon
- Mint leaves (optional)
- Fresh cranberries (optional)
- 3 (32-ounce) bottles cranberry-juice cocktail, any variety
- 2 (6-ounce) cans frozen lemonade concentrate
- 1 1/2 cups cold water
- 4 (12-ounce) cans ginger ale, chilled

The night or morning before serving, place a 12-count muffin tin on a large, rimmed baking sheet. Slice the lemon and orange into 1/4-inch-thick slices. Cut each slice in half and place 1 or 2 slices in the bottom of each muffin cup. Add 1 or 2 mint leaves and a few cranberries, if using. Pour cranberry juice cocktail over the fruit to fill each muffin cup about three-fourths full.

Carefully transfer the filled muffin cups on the baking sheet to the freezer.

Shortly before serving, make the punch by mixing lemonade and water in a large pitcher. Pour in remaining cranberry juice and stir well. Transfer mixture to a punch bowl. Just before serving, add ginger ale. Remove ice disks from freezer. Turn the muffin tin upside down and release disks onto baking sheet. If needed, you can run a bit of hot water over the tin to loosen the disks. Float the ice disks in the punch and serve immediately.

Siegfried's Seven-Layer Bars

Makes 2 dozen

- *1 cup flaked, sweetened coconut*
- *9 whole graham crackers*
- *½ cup butter, melted*
- *1 cup pecans, chopped*
- *1 cup semisweet chocolate chips*
- *½ cup white chocolate chips*
- *½ cup butterscotch chips*
- *1 (14-ounce) can sweetened condensed milk*

Preheat oven to 350 degrees F. Spread coconut on a rimmed baking sheet and toast in oven for 10 minutes. Ask an adult to remove the pan and toss the coconut once or twice while it toasts. When coconut is golden brown, remove from oven and set aside.

Coat a 9 x 13-inch baking pan with nonstick cooking spray. Place crackers in a ziplock bag and use a rolling pin to crush crackers. Pour into a bowl and toss with melted butter. Spread crumbs evenly in the bottom of prepared pan. Sprinkle pecans, chips, and coconut over the crumbs. Pour sweetened condensed milk evenly over the top.

Bake 25 to 30 minutes, until bars are golden brown. Let cool at least 2 hours before cutting into bars.

Rothbart's
Dark Chocolate Brownies

Makes 12 to 18 brownies

- 1 cup plus
  2 tablespoons flour
- 3/4 teaspoon salt
- 1/3 cup unsweetened
  dark-chocolate or
  regular cocoa powder
- 2/3 cup white sugar
- 2/3 cup brown sugar
- 1 teaspoon vanilla
- 2/3 cup vegetable oil
- 3 eggs
- 1/2 cup white
  chocolate chips
- 1/2 cup semisweet
  chocolate chips
- 1/2 cup chopped pecans
  or walnuts (optional)

Preheat oven to 350 degrees F. Grease a 9 x 9-inch square baking pan.

In a large bowl, whisk together flour, salt, cocoa powder, and sugars. Add vanilla, vegetable oil, and eggs and beat by hand or with an electric mixer until combined. Stir in chips and nuts, if using.

Pour batter into the prepared pan and bake 25 to 30 minutes, until a toothpick inserted two inches from the edge of the pan comes out with a few crumbs.

The Little Swans'
Sweet Bites

Serves 8

- 8 (8-ounce) clear glasses or plastic cups
- 6 homemade or purchased brownies
- 2 (3-ounce) packages chocolate instant pudding
- 2 cups heavy cream
- 3 tablespoons sugar
- 5 or 6 Skor bars

Break three of the brownies into bite-sized pieces and divide evenly between the 8 glasses. Prepare pudding mixes according to package directions. Layer $1/4$ cup pudding over the brownies in each glass.

In a large bowl, whip cream and sugar together with an electric mixer on high speed until soft peaks form. Spoon $1/4$ cup whipped cream over the pudding in each glass.

Place Skor bars in a large ziplock bag. Seal the bag, and then use a wooden rolling pin to crush the bars into pieces.

Sprinkle a generous spoonful of broken candy bars over the whipped cream in each glass.

Repeat layers to use remaining brownies, pudding, whipped cream, and candy bar topping. Can be served immediately, but tastes best if chilled in refrigerator a few hours before serving.

Odette and Odile's
Black-and-White Cookies

Makes 2 to 3 dozen

- *1 1/2 cups butter,
  room temperature*
- *1 cup sugar*
- *1 teaspoon vanilla*
- *3 1/4 cups flour*
- *1/4 teaspoon salt*
- *8 ounces semisweet
  chocolate*
- *2 teaspoons shortening*

Preheat oven to 350 degrees F. In a large bowl, mix butter and sugar together with an electric mixer until just combined. Do not overmix. Add vanilla and mix until just combined. Add flour and salt and mix at low speed until dough comes together. Stop mixing while dough is still somewhat crumbly.

Dump dough onto a floured surface and shape into a round disk. Wrap disk in plastic and refrigerate for 30 minutes or longer.

Divide chilled dough into 2 sections. Roll first section 1/4 inch thick and cut out cookies with a 2- to 3-inch round cookie cutter. Repeat with second section of dough.

Bake on ungreased cookie sheets for 12 to 15 minutes, until edges start to brown a little.

Cool to room temperature. Line 2 baking sheets with parchment paper and set aside.

Once cookies are cool, have an adult help you bring a pot of water to a simmer over medium heat. Break chocolate into pieces and place in a medium glass bowl. Add shortening and place bowl over the pot of simmering water. Make sure the water doesn't boil or touch the bowl.

continued

Stir chocolate occasionally, until it is smooth and melted. Remove chocolate from simmering water. Dip half of each cookie into the chocolate. Tip each cookie as needed to help chocolate spread evenly to coat the cookie half. Place dipped cookie on parchment paper to set. Let the chocolate set at room temperature about 1 hour before serving, or place in the refrigerator if you want the chocolate to harden more quickly

Swan Lake
Homemade Marshmallows

Serves 6 to 8

- 3 envelopes Knox gelatin
- 1/2 cup cold water
- 2 cups sugar
- 2/3 cup light corn syrup
- 1/4 cup water
- 1/4 teaspoon salt
- 2 teaspoons vanilla
- Powdered sugar for dusting
- 16 ounces Ghirardelli semisweet chocolate
- 4 teaspoons shortening

NOTE: This recipe isn't hard to make, but it does take a little more time than the others in this book.

The night before serving, line a rimmed baking sheet with a piece of parchment paper. Spray generously with nonstick cooking spray and set aside.

Sprinkle gelatin in the bowl of an electric stand mixer fitted with whisk attachment. Cover with 1/2 cup water and set aside to soften.

Combine sugar, corn syrup, and 1/4 cup water in a small saucepan. Heat to boiling over medium-high heat, then let mixture boil vigorously for 1 1/2 minutes. Ask an adult to help you turn stand mixer to low speed and slowly pour in the hot syrup. Once combined, add the salt, then increase the mixer speed to high and beat for 12 minutes. Mixture will become shiny and fluffy.

At the 12-minute mark, add vanilla and mix to combine.

Brush a rubber spatula with vegetable oil, and then scrape the marshmallow mixture onto the prepared pan. Use the spatula or clean, wet hands to smooth the top.

Let mixture rest, uncovered, overnight.

The next day, dust the top with powdered sugar.

Cut marshmallows into squares with scissors or use a fun-shaped cookie cutter to cut out shapes. Place shapes on a cookie sheet lined with parchment paper and place

continued

in freezer for one hour. Marshmallows can be stored in an airtight container up to a week before dipping in chocolate.

When ready to dip marshmallows in chocolate, have an adult help you bring a pot of water to a simmer over medium heat. Break chocolate into pieces and place in a medium glass bowl. Add shortening and place bowl over the pot of simmering water. Make sure the water doesn't boil or touch the bowl.

Stir chocolate occasionally, until it is smooth and melted. Remove chocolate from simmering water.

Remove marshmallows from freezer. Using a pair of tongs or holding with your fingers, dredge marshmallow shapes, one at a time, in chocolate, then return to parchment-lined baking sheet. Don't worry if chocolate doesn't completely cover the marshmallows. Part of the fun, is the homemade look you'll have when finished.

Let chocolate-covered marshmallows set up in the refrigerator for about 20 minutes—or longer—before serving. Store leftover dipped marshmallows in the refrigerator up to 3 days.

Odette's
Orange-Mango Smoothie

Serves 4 to 6

- 1 cup frozen mango pieces
- 1 cup frozen strawberries
- 1 small banana
- 3/4 cup orange juice
- 1 1/2 cups vanilla yogurt
- 1 tablespoon honey
- 1 orange, sliced, for garnish

Add all ingredients, except orange, to a blender and mix well until smooth. Pour smoothie into glasses and garnish each glass with an orange slice.

Collect Them All!